Copyright © 2022 by Symone Smith

All rights reserved. No part of this publication may be reproduced, distributed, or transmitted in any form or by any means, including photocopying, recording, or other electronic or mechanical methods, without the prior written permission of the publisher, except in the case brief quotations embodied in critical reviews and other noncommercial uses permitted by copyright law.

ISBN: 978-1-63945-290-3 (Paperback)
      978-1-63945-291-0 (Hardback)
      978-1-63945-292-7 (E-book)

The views expressed in this book are solely those of the author and do not necessarily reflect the views of the publisher, and the publisher hereby disclaims any responsibility for them.

Writers' Branding
1800-608-6550
www.writersbranding.com
orders@writersbranding.com

To my wonderful son Eddie, the world is always yours.
"I am smart. Yes, I am smart. I can read yes, I can."

Aa

I saw an Aardvark.

Did you see the Aardvark? What letter does Aardvark start with?

Aa

Aadvarks eat ants and termites. Great breakfast is it time for lunch yet?

Bb

I saw a Bear. Did you see a Bear? What letter does Bear start with?

Bb

Bears eat salmon, yum. All bears are not good climbers, how about that.

Cc

I saw a Cheetah. Did you see a Cheetah? What letter does Cheetah start with?

Cc

Cheetah's speed can increase from 0 to over 80 mph. Wow! That's fast right.

Dd

I saw a Dragonfly. Did you see a Dragonfly? What letter does Dragonfly start with?

Dd

Dragonflies eat mosquitoes. Now I didn't even know that. Did you know that?

Ee

I saw an Eagle. Did you see an Eagle? What letter does Eagle start with?

Ee

Howe's my eyesight? I have excellent vision ranked 20/5 that mean, I can spot my dinner two miles away.

Ff

I saw a Ferret. Did you see a Ferret? What letter does Ferret start with?

Ff

_____

Do not feed me fruit especially BANANAS, it will cause my stomach to hurt. Can you eat fruit?

Gg

I saw a Gar. Did you see a Gar? What letter does Gar start with?

Gg

Where am I located? Look up the answer together for more fun.

Hh

I saw a Hedgehog. Did you see Hedgehog? What letter does Hedgehog start with?

Hh

How do I protect myself? Quills. Do you notice something missing? Fill it in.

Ii

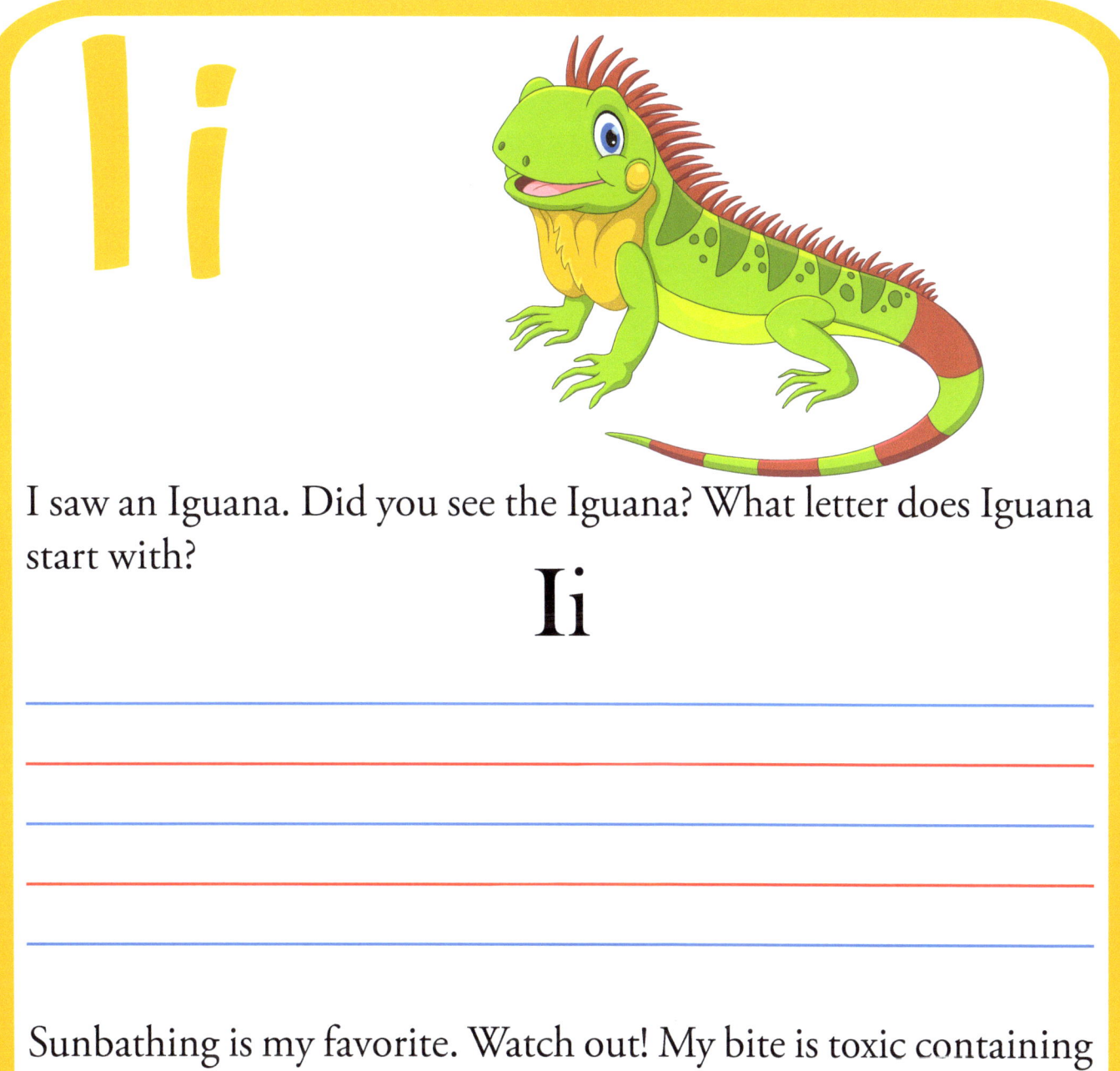

I saw an Iguana. Did you see the Iguana? What letter does Iguana start with?

Ii

Sunbathing is my favorite. Watch out! My bite is toxic containing "SALMONELLA!"

Jj

I saw a Jaguar. Did you see a Jaguar? What letter does Jaguar start with?

Jj

I can hold my breath under water for 20 minutes.

Kk

I saw Kinkajou. Did you see the Kinkajou? What letter does Kinkajou start with?

Kk

Where do I live? Tropical Forests of Central and South America. Wow! Your smart.

L l

I saw a Loris.

Did you see a Loris? What letter does Loris start with?

Ll

What do I eat? I am an omnivore. I eat bugs and small reptiles.

Mm

I saw a Mamba. Runnnn.
We made it safe. What letter does Mamba start with?

Mm

I am the longest snake in Africa. I am the most venomous too.
What punctuation mark is missing?

Nn

I saw a Narwhal. Did you see the Narwhal? What letter does Narwhal start with?

Nn

Narwhals live in the Arctic. The long pointy tusk you see is my tooth, I use it to catch fish. Bllblullbu, excuse me, I'm full now.

Oo

I saw an Opossum. Did you see the Opossum?

Oo

Wait, that starts with the letter O.

Pp

I saw a Pelican. Did you see the Pelican? What letter does Pelican start with?

Pp

What is the state bird of Louisiana? Pelican.

Qq

I saw a Quoll. Did you see a Quoll? What letter does Quoll start with?

Qq

Where am I from?

Western Australia my habitat includes forests, woodlands, and rainforest.

Rr

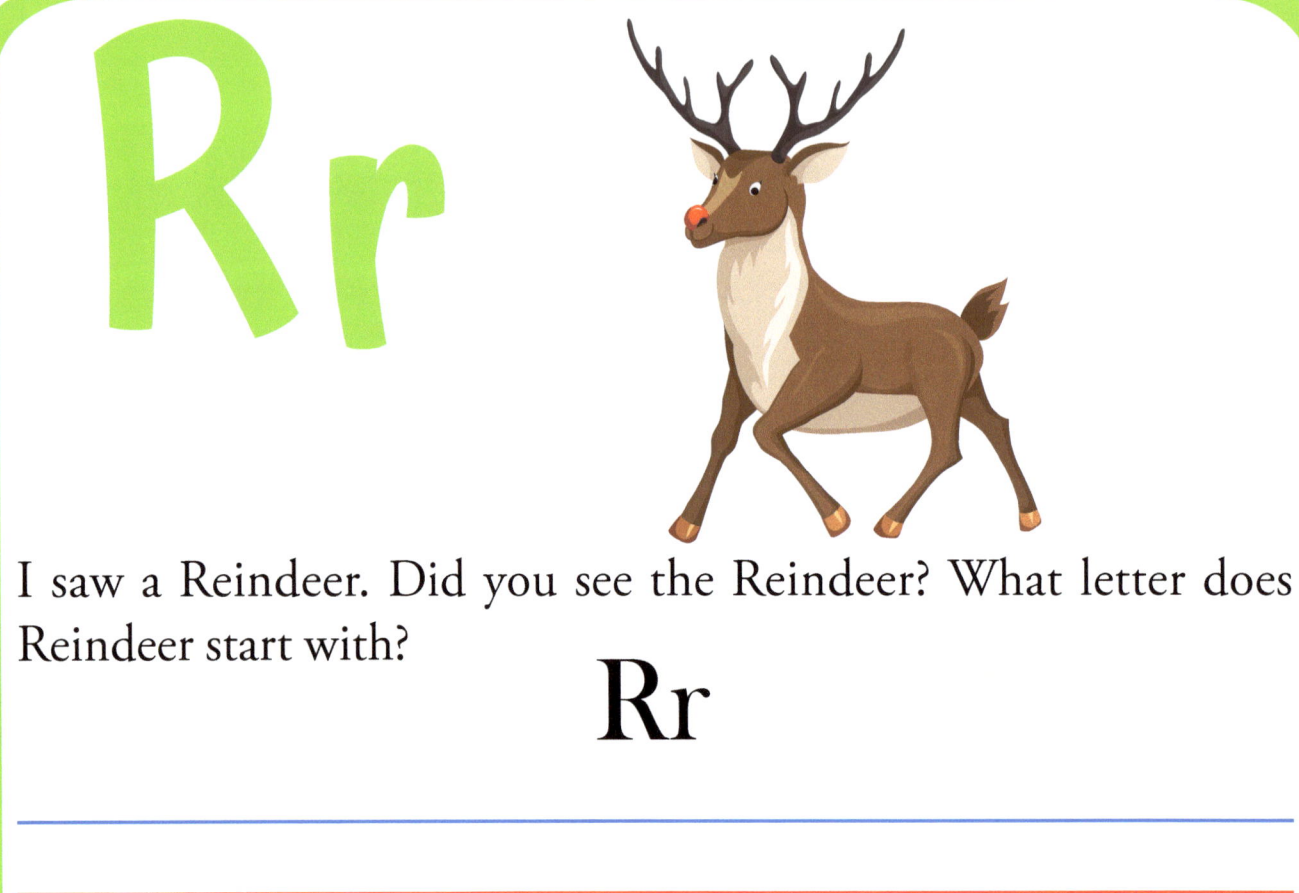

I saw a Reindeer. Did you see the Reindeer? What letter does Reindeer start with?

Rr

Where am I from? Eurasia, Europe, and North America.

Ss

I saw a Sawfish. Did you see the Sawfish? What letter does Sawfish start with?

Ss

I use my saw to pin the prey down, repositioning my prey before biting into it. My saw detects live prey in the water.

Tt

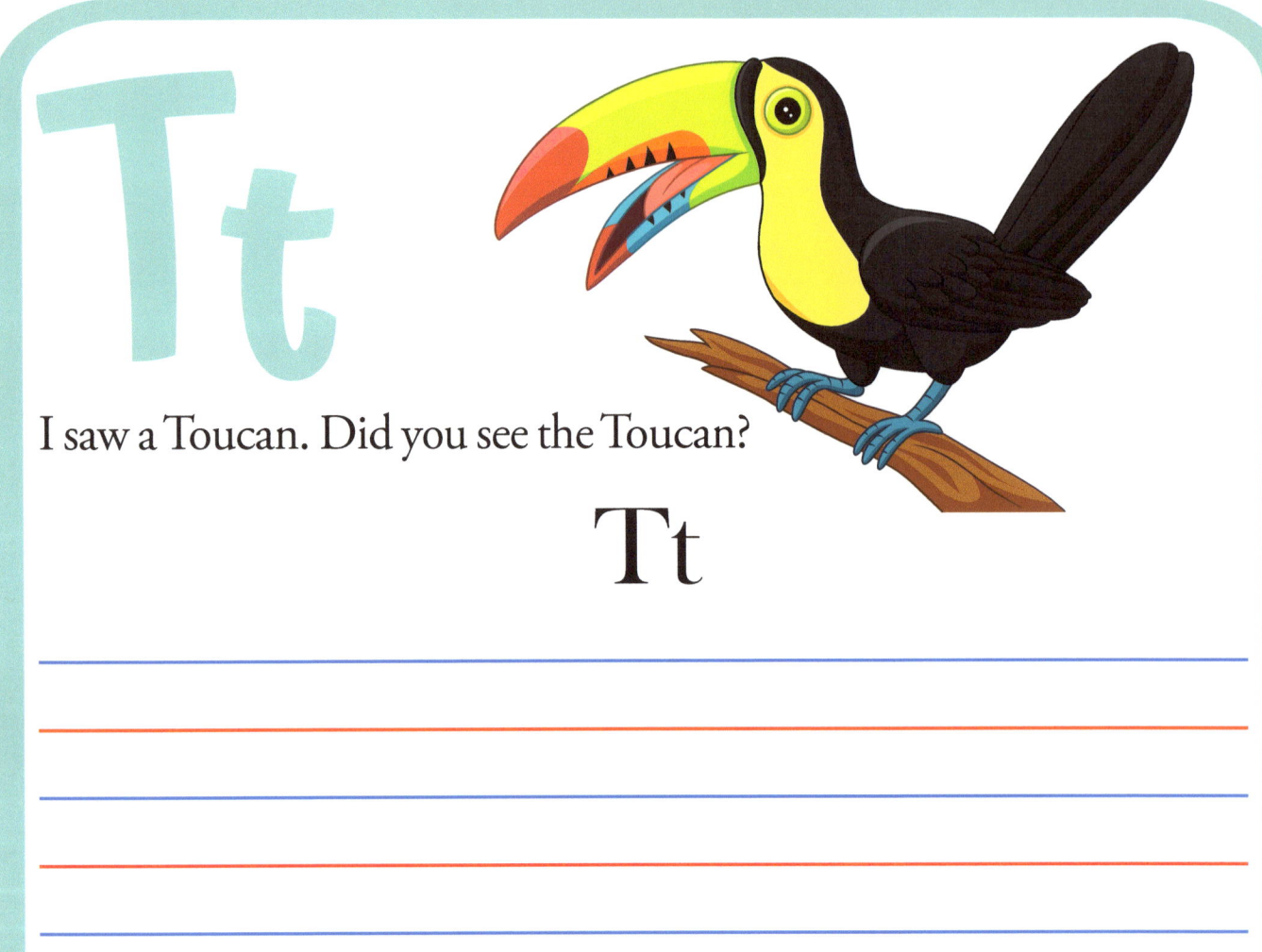

I saw a Toucan. Did you see the Toucan?

Tt

Can you name the colors on the Toucan's bill? The Toucan's bright colors are to help him attract a mate. Where else do you see a Toucan? Fruit Loop cereal hahaha.

Uu

I saw a Unau. Did you see the Unau? What letter does Unau start with?

Uu

Unau's live in Tropical Forests in South America, East Andes Colombia, Ecuador, Amazon base in Brazil. Two-toed how many toes do you have? Let's count.

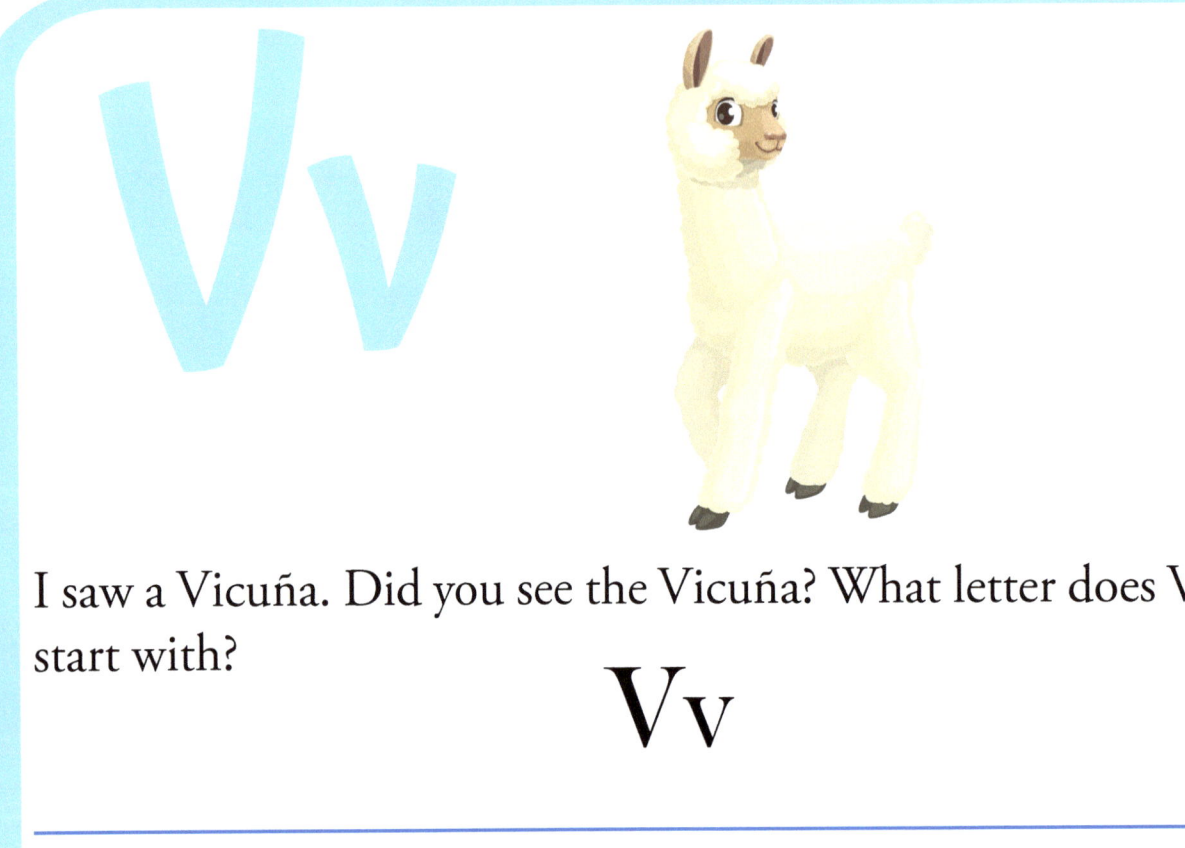

I saw a Vicuña. Did you see the Vicuña? What letter does Vicuña start with?

Vv

The mark over the n means it's a Spanish word. Vicuñas native to central Andes in South America. They are found in Peru, Northwestern Argentina Bolivia, and Northern Chile. Vicuñas are small in size.

I saw a Wombat. Did you see the Wombat? What letter does Wombat start with?

Wombats are endangered by overgrazing. Only 315 Wombats are left.

Xx

I saw a Xylocopa. Did you see the Xylocopa? What letter does Xylocopa start with?

Xx

A carpenter Bee is my common name. I love flowering plants, feeding on nectar, and collecting pollen.

I saw a Yak. Did you see the Yak? What letter does Yak start with?

Yaks live in China in the mountains. Yaks like eating grass. Yaks use their horns to break through the snow. Do you notice anything different?

Zz

I saw a Zokor. Did you see the Zokor? What letter does Zokor start with?

Zz

Zokors live in Asia. Zokors have big teeth used to cut through the roots of plants under the ground do not hibernate. More active during the spring. Rewrite the sentence correctly.

About the Author

Symone Smith is a humanitarian and a wonderful mother, devoting time towards growing and expanding education. *I Can Read* is for all children to gain an exceptional learning experience. Each page is filled with excitement while learning to appreciate the values of ncw things in life.

www.ingramcontent.com/pod-product-compliance
Lightning Source LLC
LaVergne TN
LVHW071652060526
838200LV00029B/441